INVENTORIED   hm 11255

917.6889
Pier

Pierce, C. Bedford.

Great Smokies.

ISSUED TO 10.95

DATE

917.6889   hm 11255
Pier

Pierce, C. Bedford.

Great Smokies.

DEMCO

GREAT SMOKIES

GALLERY BOOKS

An Imprint of W. H. Smith Publishers Inc.

112 Madison Avenue
New York City 10016

This edition first published in U.S.
in 1990 by Gallery Books,
an imprint of W.H. Smith Publishers, Inc.
112 Madison Avenue, New York, New York 10016

ISBN 0-8317-8832-1

Printed and bound in Spain

For rights information about the photographs in
this book please contact:

The Image Bank
111 Fifth Avenue, New York, NY 10003

Producer: Solomon M. Skolnick
Author: C. Bedford Pierce
Design Concept: Lesley Ehlers
Designer: Ann-Louise Lipman
Editor: Joan E. Ratajack
Production: Valerie Zars
Photo Researcher: Edward Douglas
Assistant Photo Researcher: Robert V. Hale
Editorial Assistant: Carol Raguso

*Title page: Morton's Overlook is near
Newfound Gap Road in Great Smoky
Mountain National Park in Tennessee.
Opposite: The 1885 Knox County
Courthouse contrasts with the ultra-
modern River Tower.*

The geologically ancient Great Smoky Mountains are the southern culmination of the Appalachian range. The 900-million-year-old rock that comprises the surface of the Smokies was once covered over by a layer of limestone sediment left behind by the receding sea 400 million years ago. When the continents of Africa and North America collided, the original rock under the limestone was thrust sharply up again, forming the mountains. With the turn of season into season, the average annual rainfall of 50 to 60 inches of precipitation, and the play of wind and water, the Smokies have been shaped and reshaped. Viewed from a distance, the mountains have gentle curves and crests, their apparent softness enhanced by the smoke-blue haze that rises from thick conifer forests and hangs over the mountains, and which likely gave them their name.

Even with 20 peaks stretching to over 6,000 feet, including the tallest, Clingman's Dome (6,643 feet), the Great Smokies do not reach above the

This page: *Knoxville, Tennessee, the "Urban Gateway" to the Great Smokies, embraces the old and the new. The River and Plaza Towers help establish Knoxville's new skyline, while the original 1786 log cabin of Knoxville's founder James White is the centerpiece of a reconstruction of his fort which served as a safe haven for travelers and settlers.*

Above: *Plaza Tower overlooks the University of Tennessee.* Below and opposite: *The Knoxville Fairgrounds was the site of the 1982 World's Fair. The Sunsphere symbolized the fair's "Energy" theme.*

timberline. At 4,500 to 6,000 feet, the mountains have the climate of a northern conifer forest. Hemlock, fir, and spruce trees, the same types found in northern New England and Canada, are remnants of a larger forest that thrived during the last Ice Age, 12,000 years ago.

Below 4,500 feet the yellow birches, maples, and beeches of a seemingly misplaced deciduous forest provide an annual flaming display of autumn colors equal to those of mid-New England. At 3,000 feet and below, the hardwoods thrive. These trees, which include some of the most extensive virgin stands in the U.S., make up the most lush temperate forests outside the American Pacific Northwest. Among the natural treasures of the Great Smokies are about 100 species of trees, 1,300 species of herbs, 2,000 types of fungi, 300 kinds of mosses, and 200 species of lichens.

Sevier County, Tennessee is Dolly Parton country. Preceding page: This statue of the singer graces Courthouse Square in Sevierville, her hometown. This page, top to bottom: At Dollywood in Pigeon Forge, the "Kinfolks" are Dolly's family who sing a blend of music from the Parton Family's roots. Exhibits at Dollywood include the carriage works. More than half of the nearly 9 million people who visit Great Smoky Mountain National Park annually enter through Gatlinburg. Following page: Flowering dogwoods at Greenbriar Cove flourish in the spring rush of the Middle Prong of the Little Pigeon River, six miles east of Gatlinburg in the national park.

This page: *The preserved grinding mill at the Alfred Duggan place and Ephraim Bales' cabin punctuate the lush hand of nature along the Roaring Fork Motor Nature Trail near Gatlinburg.*

This page: *The Roaring Fork Nature Trail passes through "The Place of a Thousand Drips" which is fed by hundreds of small streams. The trail leads back to town along the rushing water course.* Following page: *Noah "Bud" Ogle's cabin is on Cherokee Orchard Road. Many of his descendants still live nearby in Gatlinburg.*

In the mid-eighteenth century, when what is today North Carolina was still a land roamed by the Cherokee, a naturalist came to these mountains and spread word of their beauty throughout the world.

William Bartram, the son of the New World's first great botanist, John Bartram, was given a commission by Dr. John Fothergill, a leading London physician. The commission gave "Billy," as he was known, an opportunity to explore the South, to draw, take notes, hunt plants, and send back to England a report on the area's wildlife. Bartram accomplished his task well, pleasing Dr. Fothergill and fueling the European passion for natural exotica from the New World.

What remains of Bartram's physical trail through the area is a historical marker near Beechertown inscribed, "William Bartram: Philadelphia Naturalist, Author exploring this area, met a Cherokee band led by their chief Attakullakulla, in May 1775 near this spot."

This page, top to bottom: *Celadine Poppy* (Chelidonium majus), *Crested Dwarf Iris* (Iris cristata), *and Catawba Rhododendron* (Rhododendron catawbiense), *are a few examples of nature's bounty.*

This page: *The young forest in the area makes it a paradise for finding and identifying some of the more than 1,500 species of wildflowers that grow in Great Smoky Mountain National Park.*

Preceding pages: *Beech and Rhododendron thrive along the Little River.* This page and opposite: *Laurel Creek Road leads to Cades Cove, an unexpected lowland surrounded by mountains, which was settled in 1821. The Cades Cove Historical District includes the Gregg-Cable house.*

*The John P. Cable grist mill in the
Historical District is still used to make
cornmeal which is now sold to visitors
during the summer season.*

Preceding page: *The Presbyterian church is one of several houses of worship on the 11-mile-long Loop Road which is the only access to the Historical District.* This page: *These musicians are participating in Old Timer's Day at Cades Cove, a twice-yearly festival of bluegrass music that is held in May and October.*

These pages: *The Tipton's house has been preserved and a replica of their cantilevered barn was made. The enclosed upper portion of the barn provided storage for perishables. The overhang offered a degree of protection for the livestock which was kept outside.*

But his journey was immortalized in 1791 with the publication of his memoirs, *The Travels of William Bartram.* In his book, he depicted 43 Cherokee towns and villages through vivid descriptions of their customs, rituals, and social structure. Bartram had fine literary company in this area; Thomas Jefferson wrote extensively about the Cherokee as well.

Until the beginning of the nineteenth century, the southern Appalachians and the surrounding valleys were the domain of the Cherokee Nation. These non-nomadic native Americans practiced slash-and-burn farming and established permanent villages near their farm sites. The nation survived the incursion of the conquistador Hernando De Soto with his 600 well-armed troops. However, in 1838, federal troops under General Winfield Scott captured thousands of Cherokees, even though their nation had been officially recognized by the U.S., and forced them to march to a reservation in Oklahoma. The Cherokee still refer to this journey as the "Trail of Tears."

This page, top to bottom: *The Appalachian Trail extends for 2,000 miles from Maine to its terminus in Georgia. 70 miles (6-8 days of hiking) of the trail follow the Tennessee-North Carolina border in Great Smoky Mountain National Park. Sign posts of varying vintages guide travelers along the longest marked foot path in the world.* Opposite: *Winter blankets the Appalachian Trail.*

Preceding page: *The play of sun and mist, which is particular to the Smokies, accents the soft lines of some of the oldest mountains on earth.* This page: *The seven-mile-long Clingman's Dome Road leads to a summit which provides spectacular views into the North Carolina portion of the park.*

Qualla Reservation in the modern town of Cherokee, North Carolina, is the largest reservation for native Americans east of Wisconsin. It is inhabited primarily by the descendants of the Cherokee who escaped the army's "roundup" by scattering into the familiar cover of the Smokies. The Oconaluftee Indian Village at the reservation, an outdoor museum, recreates Cherokee forebears' lifestyle of 225 years ago through demonstrations of authentic crafts and techniques.

With the Cherokee Nation in effect removed from the rich lowland valleys, the movement of white settlers who had begun to arrive in the late eighteenth century became intensified and their claim to the area more secure. Newcomers arriving in the latter part of the nineteenth century found the most fertile areas already occupied and had to content themselves with homesteads on the more difficult, steeper slopes.

Preceding page: *The early morning sun burns away the mist on top of Clingman's Dome.* These pages: *The extensive logging that preceded the creation of the national park greatly diminished the habitat for wildlife in this area. White-tail deer* (Odocoileus virginianus) *and Black bears* (Ursus americanus) *have benefited from the subsequent protection of this wilderness. An occasional mountain lion* (Felis concolor) *can also be seen.*

The stability of this farming society was disrupted by the coming of the large timber companies, which saw in the Great Smokies one of the last great forests in the East. As the settlers had displaced the Cherokees, the timber companies displaced large numbers of farmers in the most fertile areas. Some families abandoned farming to take paying jobs for the lumber companies, whose ongoing need for timber destroyed much of the land. The resulting severe erosion made farming nearly impossible for those farmers who remained. By 1925, less than 100 years after the Trail of Tears, the only large uncut forests that remained were in the steep valleys and on the high ridges.

Horace Souers Kephart, a St. Louis librarian specializing in western Americana, went to the Great Smokies in 1904. Kephart's main purpose in traveling there was to restore his health amid the beauty and tranquility of the

Preceding page: *A black bear in a tree is not an uncommon sight here, nor are the stories of hungry bears dining on the contents of a careless hiker's backpack unfounded.* This page: *Alum Cave Bluffs provides welcome shelter along this steep trail to the peak of Mt. LeConte near Newfound Gap Road.* Right: *The sign beneath the overhang of Alum Cave Bluffs has become a popular place for hikers to leave their mark while preparing for their three-mile journey to the top of Mt. LeConte.*

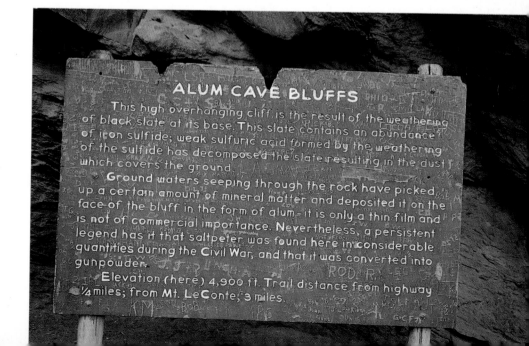

ALUM CAVE BLUFFS

This high overhanging cliff is the result of the weathering of black slate at its base. This slate contains an abundance of iron sulfide; weak sulfuric acid formed by the weathering of the sulfide has decomposed the slate resulting in the dust which covers the ground.

Ground waters seeping through the rock have picked up a certain amount of mineral matter and deposited it on the face of the bluff in the form of alum—it is only a thin film and is not of commercial importance. Nevertheless, a persistent legend has it that saltpeter was found here in considerable quantities during the Civil War, and that it was converted into gunpowder.

Elevation (here) 4,900 ft. Trail distance from highway ¼ miles; from Mt. LeConte, 3 miles.

Preceding page and this page, top: *Five trails—Alum Cave Bluffs, Boulevard, Bullhead, Rainbow Falls, and Trilliam Gap—lead to and from the summit of Mt. LeConte. Bottom: Mountains in winter as seen from Newfound Gap Road, the only road across the mountains from Gatlinburg to Cherokee.*

Sunrise as seen from Newfound Gap, the site where President Franklin Delano Roosevelt dedicated the park in 1940.

These pages: *"Tub-style" Mingus Mill is located off the Newfound Gap Road near the Oconoluftee Pioneer-Farmstead. The mill operates from May through October. Workers at the Pioneer-Farmstead visitor's center demonstrate traditional methods of farming and animal husbandry.*

great mountains and magical forests. For himself he accomplished that. For a larger cause, he helped ignite awareness of the special nature of the Smokies, a nature that he saw the lumber companies cutting and shipping out of the region. Kephart's *Our Southern Highlanders* and Margaret Morley's *The Carolina Mountains* were both published in 1913, helping to bring to a larger public an awareness of the natural and human treasures that were nurtured in these mountains and were in peril of being lost.

Kephart, Morley, and Bartram were not the only ones to fall in love with this area. George Washington Vanderbilt, the grandson of railroad magnate Cornelius Vanderbilt, purchased over 120,000 acres of land on which he built his estate, Biltmore House. Richard Morris Hunt, the famous eastern architect, designed the 250-room house, which was modeled on a French chateau and completed in 1895. Frederick Law Olmstead, creator of New York City's Central Park,

Opposite: *The town of Cherokee, North Carolina, near the southern entrance to Great Smoky Mountain National Park, is part of the Qualla Boundary Cherokee Indian Reservation, the largest reservation east of Wisconsin.* This page, top to bottom: *Tribal dance competitions are held annually in August, and the Cherokee Indian Fall Festival is held each October in the Qualla Reservation. Souvenir shops abound on Cherokee's main streets. At the Oconoluftee Indian Village, visitors can see artisans, like this one creating a dugout canoe with fire and an axe, using traditional Cherokee techniques.*

This page and opposite: *The Blue Ridge Parkway, the longest scenic drive in the world, is 469 miles long. At mile marker 417, the Cherry Cove Overlook offers a clear view of the 400-foot granite cliff known as Looking Glass Rock.*

The Biltmore House, a 250-room French Renaissance Chateau, is the largest private residence in the U.S. Designed by Richard Morris Hunt for George Vanderbilt, construction of the house was completed in 1895, five years after it was begun.

designed the 17 acres of gardens. Today, parts of the mansion, which houses works by such masters as August Renoir and Albrecht Dürer, as well as many of the original farm buildings, are open to the public.

Moses H. Cone, a North Carolina textile manufacturer, also built a mansion in these mountains. His 3,500-acre estate, donated by his heirs to the National Park Service, includes bridle paths and walking trails around two lakes. The mansion itself, Flat Top Manor, now houses a crafts center.

However, these huge estates are the exception rather than the rule and, for the most part, what is left to us today is William Bartram's legacy come into full flower:

This page, top: The Biltmore House was hand-tooled from native limestone. Bottom: Frederick Law Olmstead, who designed New York's Central Park, created and maintained 17 acres of gardens surrounding the house. Opposite: The stables stand on what was once Vanderbilt's 130,000-acre estate.

the richness of natural life—flora, fauna, and human—that dwelt in the area only later to be known as the Great Smoky Mountains.

The national parks in the American West, such as Yellowstone and Yosemite, were on land either owned or accessible to the federal government. Establishing a great park in the East was a different challenge. Neither the federal government nor the recently formed (1916) National Park Service were prepared to purchase land for the park. People such as Kephart publicized and gathered general support and donations to acquire the necessary land needed from the farmers and the lumber companies. Donations from schoolchildren were as wel-

This page, top: *The library includes over 20,000 volumes which sit beneath a painted ceiling brought from the Pisani Palace in Venice, Italy.* Bottom: *George Vanderbilt's collection of automobiles is impressive enough to be a museum unto itself.* Opposite: *The indoor winter garden includes a sunken marble floor, fine sculpture, and a lavish fountain.*

This page: *The scenery just outside of Asheville, North Carolina is among the most soothing along the route of the Blue Ridge Parkway.*

come and encouraged as the $5 million grant received from John D. Rockefeller, Jr.

The authorization to develop the park finally came in 1934. It was dedicated at Newfound Gap by President Franklin Delano Roosevelt in 1940.

The 520,000-acre Great Smoky Mountain National Park is visited by 9 million people each year, more than any other national park in the country. More than half of these visitors enter through Gatlinburg, a mountain resort town on the Tennessee side of the park.

Deep thickets of heath, flame azaleas, and rhododendrons blaze with color in the late spring and early summer. In the forests, a profusion of wildflowers, of which some 1,500 species have been identified, bloom from March through June. Bird-foot violet, bishop's cap, bluets, bleeding heart, Catesby's trillium, wild strawberry, Dutchman's breeches, foamflowers, and gaywings are just a sampling of the species found in the park. The Bud Ogle Nature Trail and the Roaring Fork

This page, top to bottom: *The passing of the day is reflected in the changing skyline of Asheville, North Carolina, whose growth and wealth was spurred by the coming of the railway in 1880 and the arrival of entrepreneurs George Vanderbilt, E. W. Grove, John D. Rockefeller, Henry Ford, and others about a decade later.*

Motor Nature Trail are two of
the most accessible places to
enjoy the delights of this
wildflower wonderland.

On a few of the high
ridges, at elevations over
5,000 feet, are the mysterious
"balds." These meadowlike
patches of grass and low
vegetation interrupt the great
stretches of forest. The origin
of the balds has been the
subject of much speculation.
Some suggest that these areas
were subjected to repeated
burning by the Cherokee to
provide an open area to which
game could be flushed from
the forest. Natural forest fires
or peculiar soil conditions are
cited as alternative reasons,
and some researchers suggest
that heavy grazing by elk and
bison contributed to the balds'

Preceding page: *The Buncombe County Courthouse is framed in this view through a
modern sculpture.* This page: *Opened as a museum in 1949, this 1883 white-framed
structure was "home" to numerous boarders when it was owned by Julia Wolfe,
mother of writer Thomas Wolfe. Wolfe's novel,* Look Homeward, Angel, *was inspired
by his mother's "Old Kentucky Home" where he lived for ten years prior to leaving
for college.*

resistance to trees rooting in areas that are otherwise densely forested.

Early settlers actually expanded the balds to serve as pastures for their cattle. Regardless of their origin, the balds have diminished in number in the twentieth century. Those which remain are maintained by rangers.

Black bears, deer, opossums, raccoons, skunks, and foxes are native inhabitants of the Smokies and can, with a little patience, be easily observed. However, the elusive mountain lion, which once roamed these mountains, has not been observed here in the last 50 years, although some people claim to have heard its chilling screams at night. The Smokies, with their rich, wet growth, are the salamander capital of North America. Approximately two dozen species, from two-inch pygmies to two-foot hellbenders, wander through the undergrowth.

Over 800 miles of walking trails, from modest loops to a 70-mile piece of the Appalachian Trail, stretch across the crests of the Smokies.

Water seems to be everywhere in the park. The almost ever-present rain feeds the many streams that descend

Preceding page: *Grandfather Mountain (at mile marker 306), is estimated to be 1 billion years old and is one of the oldest rock formations on earth.* This page, top to bottom: *A clear view from the Blue Ridge Parkway near Grandfather Mountain is somewhat unusual in this land of mist. The sights along the parkway include the view from Wolf Mountain. This nearby pastoral farm is only one example of the variety of views from the parkway.*

The air rushing through the valley below Blowing Rock will actually carry light objects upward for a short distance, giving the appearance that the objects are indeed defying gravity.

Moses H. Cone, a North Carolina textile manufacturer, known as the "Blue Denim King" had an impressive view of his 3,600-acre estate from the heights of Flat Top Mountain. The materials needed to build his home, Flat Top Manor, were drawn up the side of the mountain by men leading teams of oxen. Overleaf: A majestic purple shade draws over the Blue Ridge Mountains.

from the summits of the mountains in trickling brooks and impressive waterfalls. The afternoon sunlight on the water of Rainbow Falls, which spills more than 80 feet, causes the rainbow effect. The Place of a Thousand Drips, a cascade of water that descends over several ledges and forms hundreds of little streams, feeds the mosses and ferns that grow there. Spraying down into an open pool, Grotto Falls is a favorite destination for hikers because a path leads behind the falls, giving those who make the trek an unusual perspective.

The park celebrates the history of the region, as well as its flora and fauna. Cades Cove Historical District appears at first to be a living town, but no lights go on in these cabins, no smoke wafts from their chimneys. However, the preserved settlement gives visitors a glimpse of a Smoky Mountains farmer's life before the park was founded.

History of another type is celebrated here as well. Twice a year, in May and October, the park hosts Old Timer's Day. Although it's primarily a bluegrass festival, a wide variety of other activities take place, from quilt shows to demonstrations of clogging, a type of dance in which the dancers wear clogs and stamp their feet in time to the music.

And lastly, of the mountains Horace Kephart said, "Nearly always there hovers over the high tops and around them, a tenuous mist, a dreamy blue haze. . . . Beyond is mystery, enchantment."

Index of Photographers

TIB indicates The Image Bank